# THIS IS
# Painted
# Desert

*by John J. Wagoner*

Former Staff Interpretive Specialist, Petrified Forest National Park

Mr. Wagoner, a career employee of the National Park Service,
is the author of both the text and poetry, as well as contributor
of many of the photographs for this book. He is a
graduate in the fields of botany, geology and public speaking
from Humboldt State College at Arcata, California.

...ociation, Petrified Forest National Park, Holbrook, Arizona 86025. L.C. number 76–157463.
...RIFIED FOREST — THE STORY BEHIND THE SCENERY is also available from the Association.

I stand and see it
I am awe-inspired by it,
   this...this...nameless place.

# The Desert

If any natural area in the world can be said to have a "personality" then it is surely true of the Painted Desert. Those who live near it and see its subtle changes throughout any particular day and throughout the seasons of the year, are caught up with the desert's beauty, are intimate with its "personality" and are witness to its various moods.

The Painted Desert expresses itself through moods which are created by the changing weather patterns. A markedly brooding effect is created by black rain clouds rolling overhead, casting the badlands as dark and foreboding; there is an aura of gaiety when puffy white clouds coast overhead creating kaleidoscopic patterns of brilliant reds against subdued reds; anger is expressed as harsh winds roar through the arroyos while one's clothing lashes stingingly against the skin; a feeling of gentleness is projected when the desert is coated blood-red at sunrise and at sunset; a feeling of boredom exists at high noon with a clear bright sky, promoting an effect of flatness and drabness; and then there is the moment of regal aloofness when the reds are draped with a cape of newly fallen snow. These are some of the Painted Desert's many moods, and they all depend on the day, the time and the weather conditions under which the desert is seen.

It is the intent of this publication to supplement your visit to the Painted Desert — to show the desert as others have seen and will see it; to present as many of its moods that it is not possible for you to have the time to see.

You will note that this is basically a picture book in conjunction with short three line poems (Japanese Haiku) to help establish various moods. Scientific and technical data is conspicuously absent because this type of information is available in the companion book PETRIFIED FOREST: THE STORY BEHIND THE SCENERY.

*Cast by an ancient river;*

*Salted with iron rich cinders;*

*Covered by the sands of time.*

*Raised by forces from under;*

*Worn away by wind and water;*

*Reddened badlands before my eyes.*

THIS IS PAINTED DESERT

Twisted Juniper
Standing as a monument
to that which has passed.

They call you badlands:
for want of a better name,
they call you badlands.

Each way that you look
you see the many patterns...
nature's fingerprints.

Blanched and cracked by sun,
forming in net-like patterns;
the dry desert soil.

Magnificently ... crimson red to deepened blue:

red desert, blue sky.

Comes the spice of life,

A silt-laden stream,
so suddenly to appear...
soon gone in the sands.

water-laden thunderstorm;     spatter of raindrops.

Heaven and desert
strung together on nature's
own water-spun web.

For but a short time
the yearlies come popping up
to delight the eye.

Indian Paintbrush

Prince's Plume

Desert Primrose

Evening Primrose

Painted Cup

Globe Mallow

Red sandy desert     filled to the brim with silence;

miles and miles of it.

There it is, hear it?
It's crashing in upon you,
the desert silence.

The wind and rain
daily scouring this land;
grows more beautiful.

Bullock's Oriole

Prairie Dog

Bullsnake

Hair, scales and feathers
of wildlife seldom seen,
but here all the same.

Juniper

The perennials,
sleepy winter, wakeful spring
year in and year out.

Rubber Rabbitbrush

Ephedra

Ragged rugged hills,
worn down by rain, wind and time;
how timeless you seem.

In one sweeping stroke
painting all in crimson red
the afternoon sun.

Pulling on the quilt
of crystalline winter snow…
the desert sleeps.